Preparing for Interviews

Shelley Burt

Pitman Publishing
128 Long Acre, London, WC2E 9AN

A Division of Longman Group UK Limited

First published in New Zealand as two books in 1989 and 1991
First published in Great Britain 1993
Reprinted 1993 (twice)

British Library Cataloguing-in-Publication Data
A catalogue record for this book is available from the British Library.

ISBN 0273 60133 4

Printed and bound in Great Britain by Bell and Bain Ltd, Glasgow

*Sincere thanks to those who have offered
positive encouragement and inspiration,
especially Alisdair Daines, Bronwen Strang,
Esme Palliser, Colin Gunn, and Judy Finn.*

Contents

Introduction

In an environment of too few jobs and too many applicants, each time we apply for vacancies we place ourselves in a situation of extreme competition. This competition has meant that Curriculum Vitaes (or resumes) and interview performance are now vital elements of the job application process. Competition also means that marketing skills *must* come into play, just as they do in the consumer market.

Part I of this book presents an innovative approach to C.V. writing, recognising the need to market oneself to employers. It is presented in an easy-to-follow format and aims to make the arduous task of preparing a C.V. as painless as possible. Whether you proceed on your own or work in a group, you will find the resultant document effective and impressive. This will do wonders for your self-confidence and ability to cope with the next phase - the interview (*see* Part II).

Going for job interviews takes effort. Not just the physical effort of getting dressed and arriving on time but also the mental effort of being prepared and confident. Knowing what to expect is part of the preparation and a key to 'interview survival'. What do employers ask? What do they look for? What form will the interview take? What questions should I ask? These are just some of the questions job seekers need to study before they face the interview.

Part II is intended as a guide for job seekers and as a resource for those interviewers who appreciate the importance of staff selection and who would like to feel confident that their methods are in tune with those of other organisations. These days it is not uncommon for companies to use personnel consultants to select staff but for those who cannot afford it, or prefer to select their own, here is a guide to how the others do it.

PART I

Preparing a Curriculum Vitae

1 What is a Curriculum Vitae?

C.V. stands for Curriculum Vitae and means the same as *resume*. It is a summary of your 'vital statistics' and work-related experience (paid and unpaid) to date. This is the bald definition but, as I have pointed out in the *Introduction*, it needs to be something more. It needs a *competitive edge*.

2 Selling yourself

Over many years of involvement with C.V.s and experience in marketing, I began to notice that the 'typical C.V.' was not responding adequately to the highly competitive labour market. Surely marketing principles could apply here, where competition abounded yet personal selling techniques were nowhere to be seen? An analogy came to mind. As job applicants struggling to impress and be noticed, are we not like products on a shelf trying to influence? And is not the employer like the buyer, who cares about packaging and wants to know what the product can do for them? And, like the buyer, the employer is influenced by *perceived benefits:* what's in it for them.

One of the main purposes of the C.V. is *to get you an interview.* You are relying on it, solely, to represent you. The key is to understand that the C.V. is a *sales document.* Because you only get one chance, you must sell yourself well.

Sell what? One of the key questions an employer will have in mind as he/she wades through job applications is "What skills does this person have to do the job?". It is the identification of skills that is the key to preparing an effective C.V. Too often C.V.s concentrate on *features* (what jobs were done) instead of *benefits* (the skills needed to do those jobs).

What is a skill? "Expertness, practised ability, facility in an action or in doing or to do something; dexterity, tact" (Oxford Dictionary). *Everyone* has skills, useful skills! School leavers, children, labourers, business people, office workers, women in the home, unemployed people.... . The key is identifying and stating them, thereby giving them value.

Finally, a C.V. is a very personal document and you should prepare one which seems best for you and the position you are seeking. This book is a *guide* - something you can adapt to suit your particular needs. Even if you already have a C.V., you will probably feel like revising it after reading *Part I*.

3 *Identifying your skills*

While some may prefer to labour alone, I believe working in groups makes the task easier. Identifying your skills is going to take time. You need to purposefully ponder over your past and in particular, allow yourself the freedom to write down whatever comes to mind, avoiding the urge to heed any negative thoughts that try to sabotage your efforts.

If you are keen to work in groups, I suggest the following format:

- Work in groups of three.

- One person talks about his/her activities over the past 12 months - what they've been doing, where, and with particular emphasis on the skills they have developed in performing their tasks.

- The second person listens and asks questions. They fossick for skills - "What did that job involve?" "What do you mean by 'looked after the place while the boss was away'?", and so on. Use the questions below to help.

- The third person is the recorder. An important task of the writer is to ensure that they write down the skill *and* the experience to which it relates. It is inadequate to say "I have organised"; you must say what you have organised, where and preferably when. Write on one side of the paper only.

What often happens in this group setting is that the very act of talking 'frees up' the speaker and much more comes to light than would otherwise. Rotate the roles until each person has spoken, then start again, this time going back over the years to the point where you feel there are no more skills to be drawn out.

To help you along, look at *all* of the groups below and use the questions to help identify your skills. Make sure you also look through those career groups that don't seem relevant to you. You may discover that you do have a particular skill but that it was used under different circumstances. Try to think of your own questions.

Parenting in the home

Have you ever -

- participated in and/or organised parent help at school?
- been a member of, or held an office such as secretary, treasurer, president on committees/societies (e.g. school committees, health groups, women's groups)?
- dealt with conflict? How? For example, by negotiating (skill), pacifying (skill), arbitrating (skill).
- supported children's activities like ballet, sports, music, school days, etc?
- adapted to change, e.g. separation, divorce, illness, crises? Emphasise the positive aspects and the ways in which you have become a stronger person.
- entertained guests/held dinner parties? What organisational and co-ordination skills did you use, as well as practical and social skills?
- motivated family members and yourself to achieve goals?
- communicated with people of all ages and occupations (e.g. public servants, school teachers, dentists, doctors, trades people, business people, teenagers and children)?
- budgeted the family income/made buying decisions?

Don't forget skills such as nursing, teaching, tolerance and nutrition! Write down your experiences in full.

Example:

As a parent, I have -

- *dealt with conflict through listening, negotiating and pacifying.*
- *organised and participated in kindergarten, which included producing a newsletter and liaising with parents and speakers.*
- *raised funds for our local school. This involved...*

and so on.

Parenting and paid employment

Look through the questions above and consider the following -

- how do you manage your time/prioritise your tasks?
- have you organised child support - what did this involve?
- how do you manage your income?

Community work

Have you ever -

- – spoken to groups?
- – taken minutes at meetings?
- – chaired/facilitated meetings/workshops?
- – held an office such as secretary, treasurer, etc?
- – counselled - one-to-one or by telephone?
- – written letters/reports/proposals/submissions?
- – liaised with other community groups?
- – organised events like conferences, open days?
- – raised funds?
- – handled enquiries?
- – run educational schemes/campaigns through schools or for the public?
- – provided support for fellow workers?

Expand on your experience and write it down in the way described under *Parenting in the home*.

Office work

Have you ever -

- – typed/filed/written documents (specify types)?
- – operated office equipment (specify)?
- – arranged travel bookings, meetings, conferences, sales promotions, product launches?
- – interviewed/hired staff?
- – have you trained staff?
- – analysed proposals/statistical data and made recommendations?
- – controlled budgets?
- – initiated new schemes or methods of working?
- – demonstrated products to people?
- – supervised staff?
- – achieved selling milestones?
- – planned sales calls/devised a sales plan...

and so on!

Labouring *(forestry, farming, mining etc.)*

Have you ever -

– handled or driven equipment? (Specify. Was it dangerous or complex to use?)
– initiated new and better methods of doing a task?
– tended and raised plants or animals? What did this entail?
– repaired and/or improved equipment?
– invented anything?
– written reports or submissions?
– devised a planting/harvesting/mining/building plan?
– marketed your produce/products?
– negotiated prices with buyers?
– motivated team members? How?
– organised equipment or stores supplies?
– solved transportation, cultivation, other problems?
– budgeted finances?
– hired staff?
– built anything?

Example:

As a Forestry worker for XYZ (1976-1982), I have -

– *tended and raised over 9,000 pinus radiata trees over a period of seven years. Inspection reports have shown an excellent average planting standard of 85%.*
– *written monthly reports to Forestry headquarters on the condition of soil in my area, making appropriate recommendations where necessary.*
– *initiated a new method of watering trees, which involves... etc.*

Personal and other services *(e.g. hairdressers, cooks, domestic help, bar assistants)*

Have you ever -

– dealt with complaints? How?
– listened to client requirements?
– created something new?
– provided after sales service?
– handled equipment (specify)?
– handled food?
– kept premises/locations clean?

- dealt with the public?
- taken part in promotions/competitions?
- inspected finished work for quality?
- hired and/or trained staff?

Example:

As a bar assistant for Hong Kong Restaurant (1977-1979), I -

- *dealt courteously with members of the public.*
- *controlled stock levels of ale.*
- *maintained clean bar facilities.*
- *handled complaints with patience and empathy.*

Factory/workshops

Have you ever -

- used equipment or tools (specify)?
- repaired equipment or tools?
- repaired/serviced vehicles or other engines?
- arranged staff functions?
- supervised staff?
- trained staff?
- improved methods of carrying out tasks?
- attended/facilitated meetings?
- assembled products?
- packaged products?
- checked products for quality?

Example:

As a factory worker for Mole Valley Pipes (1963-1979), I -

- *checked products for quality as part of my duties as Quality Control Officer.*
- *used a wide variety of factory equipment such as ...*
- *trained junior staff on job techniques and demonstrated the use of machinery.*
- *assisted in organising staff functions, which involved booking venues, promoting the function by way of newsletter and posters, and arranging food and entertainment.*

Transport *(e.g. taxis, freight carriers, fork-lift drivers, etc.)*

Have you ever -

- scheduled work to meet deadlines?
- operated machinery?
- given prompt and courteous service?
- repaired machinery?
- budgeted?
- dealt with complaints?

Expand on your experiences using the same format as for previous headings.

Professional and technical

Have you ever -

- managed people?
- motivated people?
- delegated tasks?
- written reports/proposals?
- negotiated fees?
- represented a client in their absence?
- tendered for work?
- planned business strategies, marketing campaigns etc?
- attended conferences, forums, meetings?
- designed anything?
- created anything?
- solved noteworthy problems?
- initiated new developments/concepts?
- formulated and controlled budgets?
- forecast sales?

and so on!

Art

Have you ever -

- drawn, sculptured, played, written, performed, potted, carved, painted, weaved, etc. Think about what this involved - not just the technical aspects but also the conceptual and abstract abilities?
- scheduled work to meet deadlines?
- marketed your work?

- spoken to groups about your work?
- written about your work?

Self-employment

Have you ever -

- set up office systems (admin, accounting, etc.)
- researched the market? How?
- identified your target market(s) and your market position?
- drawn up a marketing plan and implemented it - how?
- attended courses on business skills?
- manufactured products?
- provided a service?
- marketed your business, products, self? How?
- budgeted/written financial plans?
- planned and scheduled activities to meet deadlines?
- negotiated prices/fees?
- formulated advertising campaigns?

and so on. Expand on your experiences in the format described previously.

Unemployment

Have you ever -

- looked for work? How? (These are job search skills).
- organised or attended meetings, say with other unemployed people?
- researched companies prior to applying for positions?
- initiated contact, i.e. 'cold-calling'? This calls for assertiveness skills and qualities such as courage and determination.
- provided support to other people, unemployed or not? How?
- investigated sources of assistance? Explain how.

Example:

As an unemployed person I have -

- *developed job search skills as a result of applying for vacancies over a period of _____ months/years.*
- *developed research skills when gaining essential background information on companies I have applied to for work.*

> – displayed assertiveness and determination in initiating contact
> with potential employers. I have called on 95 businesses in the last
> year and, although no vacancies existed, their response to my
> approach was positive and encouraging.

School/tertiary experience

Have you ever -

– been involved in team sports (then you have skills such as giving
and taking instructions and working in a team)?
– been on committees, councils, groups either as participant or
office-holder?
– organised sports or gala days, trips, concerts etc?
– been a prefect, head girl/boy?
– spoken to a group of people - e.g. delivered a paper?
– been consistently punctual to class?
– researched topics for assignments - explain what you did, e.g.
researched literature (library), interviewed people, evaluated
information etc?
– analysed information/statistics? Explain to what end, e.g. "with the
aim of making recommendations to ...".
– had holiday jobs - think about what you used, did, sold?
– worked in groups on a project?
– counselled other students?
– written reports, assignments?
– sat exams?
– formulated a study plan?
– met assignment deadlines?

Expand on your experiences, following the format in preceding
examples.

To make sure you haven't overlooked anything, look at each of the
following words in the Skills Register and ask yourself whether you
have ever used that skill in any of the jobs or roles you have had (paid
or unpaid). Think about each job/role individually and note down next
to the word the experience you had and the tasks carried out, even if it
was as far back as school days. Think about responsibilities you have
accepted in clubs, committees, groups, holiday jobs.

Some words won't conjure any memories. Leave them and move to the
next word. Use a dictionary to clarify meanings of words you don't
know. Add your own words to the list and don't be afraid to put down
the 'marginal' experiences - you can weed out later.

SKILLS REGISTER *

Administered	Liaised
Analysed	Made
Arranged	Marketed
Assembled	Managed
Budgeted	Motivated
Built	Negotiated
Cared for	Operated
Classified	Organised
Contributed to	Performed
Controlled	Persuaded
Co-ordinated	Pioneered
Created	Piloted
Demonstrated	Planned
Designed	Prepared
Edited	Promoted
Evaluated	Published
Forecast	Recruited
Grew	Repaired
Guided	Researched
Handled	Scheduled
Helped	Secured
Hired	Set up
Implemented	Sold
Improved	Solved
Initiated	Supervised
Inspected	Spoken (publicly)
Interviewed	Taught
Invented	Tested
Investigated	Trained
Judged	Verified
Kept the Books	Won
Listened	Written

By now you'll be astounded at the number and variety of skills you have to sell! In fact, you may be feeling a bit panic-stricken at the wad of paper you have collected. There will be a lot of duplication and, although I have stressed the importance of expanding the experience to which the skill relates, there is a limit and you must use your discretion to arrive at a statement which is concise and informative.

It is important to understand in going through this exercise that your skills are *transferable*. If you've researched before, you have that skill and can use it again. It is also vital to avoid overemphasising facts (features) about your past. Instead, concentrate on the skills and abilities (benefits) associated with all your work experiences.

The next step is to take a pair of scissors and some sellotape. The task is to group your skills under suitable headings. This is done to make it easier for the reader to digest the information. You might, for instance, have skills that relate to community work, or management of a business, or being at school, starting a business, and so on. Some possible headings to group your skills under might be - Organisational Experience, Supervisory Experience, Business Management Experience, Training Course Experience, School Experience. Appropriate headings will suggest themselves once you have grouped like skills together.

Weed out skills you feel are no longer relevant, perhaps because they have been superseded by higher achievements, not because it's been a few years since you have used them. Sometimes you may have the same skills appearing under different groups. See if you can either delete them from one group or put two groups together under one heading - e.g. 'Community Work Experience' and 'Supervisory Experience' might become 'Community & Supervisory Experience'. You may also find that the skills under a group relate to more than one job. In that case you could introduce the skills by saying, "As a Sales Assistant for XYZ Company (1972-75) and a Branch Manager for ABC Company (1976-82), I
have ...". Or you could have subheadings under the group name. It really depends on your particular circumstances and needs. And a good tip is to go away and leave it for an hour or two if you find it's not coming together; a fresh perspective can often find an easy solution.

4 *Putting it together*

Although your grouped skills form the major part of your C.V., there are also other areas which must be covered.

Start your C.V. with the centred heading: CURRICULUM VITAE, then follow the suggested format below. Note that we are not yet talking about presentation, only content and which headings go where. You might decide, for instance, on a title page with 'Curriculum Vitae' in large lettering inside a striking border (refer to Chapter 8: *Presentation*).

NAME: (First, Middle, Last)

ADDRESS: (If PO Box, give street address as well)

TELEPHONE: (Home/work. Give area code if appropriate)

DATE OF BIRTH: (Also give age in brackets, e.g. 28 February 1960 (29 years))

NATIONALITY: (Optional) If your place of birth was not the United Kingdom, include details of permanent residency or work permits.

MARITAL STATUS: (Optional)

DEPENDANTS: (Optional)

HEALTH: (Optional) Normally stated as "Excellent" or "Good" unless you suffer a disability or sickness which may affect your performance.

PERSONAL SKILLS & ABILITIES: (First major heading) - This is where your grouped skills go. And they appear now because you need to get the best up front. Depending on the job in question, put the groups and skills in order of importance (i.e. importance to the *reader*). Focus on the job requirements. This is tailoring your C.V. to the job, just as you would tailor an advertisement to the target audience. You may also want to leave some skills that are not relevant to the position out altogether. However, if you are unsure, leave them in.

Set out your skills, under each group heading, in the way shown in the examples under *Identifying Skills* and in the sample C.V. further on in *Part I*. Write concisely.

EMPLOYMENT HISTORY: (Next major heading) - Because we have thoroughly covered experience and tasks under the previous heading, all that is required here are dates worked at each job, title of the position held, and name and address of employer.

These are listed most recently to earliest because, from a selling standpoint, you want the reader to switch in immediately to your current level of achievement. For most this is greater now than when their work record first began. Always get the best up front. Always think about the reader.

Example

1988 to present	Personal Secretary to General Manager of ABC Personnel Consultants, P.O. Box 123, Marlborough, Wilts 1BX 4HT.
1986-1988	Secretary to Marketing Manager, National Westminster Bank, Private Bag 234, Swindon, Wilts 1HT 3BC.
1983-1986	Clerk/Typist, Burford Borough Council, P.O. Box 3, Burford, Wilts 4BT 1CH.

EDUCATION: Again, the most recent first. If you had tertiary education, only go back as far as secondary school. If secondary school was the limit of your formal education, go back as far as primary school.

State the name and address of the school or institution, years in attendance and qualifications and awards gained. Also include any involvement on school committees, etc. if not already mentioned. For tertiary qualifications attach a separate sheet of subjects and grades.

You will have to use discretion in deciding what is relevant. Primary school swimming certificates, for example, would not be relevant unless you were applying for a position for which such certificates were in some way important. However awards for work attitude, like diligence or working without supervision for example, are worth retaining as some employers feel that work habits acquired in school days are likely to be repeated in later years.

Do not forget to mention night classes or correspondence courses you have undertaken. These demonstrate your openness to on-going education and a desire for growth.

If you have attended numerous training courses, workshops, seminars, etc you could include these under a separate heading, listing them along with the year and location.

PERSONAL OBJECTIVES: This is optional. You may wish to write a statement of your career aims. This can include what you would like to achieve in the position you are seeking and how you would see your role.

PROFESSIONAL MEMBERSHIPS AND AWARDS: If you have a number of awards/memberships to organisations, have a separate heading for them. Include the name of the organisations, your role/position in them and also any awards you have gained.

INTERESTS: This is not the place to write screeds of narrative on your pet hobby! The reader is probably keen to see the end by now, so make it easy for them. Just list the clubs/organisations you belong to, along with the position held if any, and the leisure activities you pursue. Note that interests are not necessarily abilities; they are things you enjoy doing or observing.

REFERENCES: List the references that are attached. If possible include local contacts for verbal references. Always check with them that they are willing to be your referee!

References should be obtained from past employers and other people who have recently been involved with you. It's also a good idea to send referees a copy of your C.V. and any information about the job in question.

Never throw references away, no matter how old.

Finally

- Always be as brief as possible. Edit harshly if your C.V. is more than four or five typed pages. There is one exception to this. Occasionally, particularly in educational areas, some vacancies are filled without interviewing. In this case you are relying *solely* on the C.V. to get you the job. It will therefore be necessary to expand on some areas and present a dynamic, visually interesting (*see* Chapter 8: *Presentation for ideas*), and very informative C.V. Editing, however, is still essential. Always be concise.

- Sign your C.V. at the end - it adds a personal touch.

- *Never* send original certificates. Get good quality photocopies. The C.V. itself however should be an original (e.g. from a word processor) and the covering letter must be an original.

- Target your C.V. to the job in question. Identify the key skills the employer is looking for and tailor your C.V. to suit. Ensure you have addressed the key skills and attributes stated in the Job Description and/or Ideal Person Specification.

- Enclosed with the C.V. will be copies of qualifications, certificates etc. Put the most recent achievements first *or* the most important for that job vacancy. Unless specifically requested, birth certificates are not required.

- Where an application form needs to be completed, fill it in and attach your C.V. *as well*. Write on the form that your C.V. is attached. You can also put "Refer attached C.V." in appropriate areas on the form, rather than repeat what's in the C.V.

5 *The job notice*

In order to tailor your covering letter (*see* next chapter) and your C.V. to the job, you need to have a clear idea of what the employer is seeking. A job description usually provides the best information and it is wise to obtain one whenever they are available. Occasionally, however, all you have to go on is the job vacancy notice. These vary widely from in-depth full descriptions, which appear to provide sufficient information to those that are sparse in outlining requirements (perhaps leading you to wonder if they really know their requirements or if they are testing you).

Let's look at a few examples of job notices to identify the key elements.

ELECTRICAL ENGINEER

(Graduate aged 25-45)

With experience in rating and selection of components associated with switchgear, concept design of motor control schemes, process controls and PLCs. Must be capable of evaluating detailed specifications. Project management experience essential. CAD experience an advantage. This is a secure, progressive appointment with excellent prospects in an expanding company. An attractive remuneration package will be offered.

Apply with detailed C.V. to Mr P A Wood, Technical Sales Director, Simple Industrial Developments Ltd, Kingdom Close, Darlington, County Durham DL2 2BL.

- The notice calls for specific technical skills in the first sentence. They have detailed these carefully and you need to demonstrate in your C.V. the experience you have obtained in these areas. You also need to reassure them in the covering letter that you have experience in all the areas they outline, highlighting any particular strengths.

- Evaluation skills are important. Again, demonstrating your experience is a must.

- Same comment for project management experience, placing slightly more emphasis on this because it is "essential".

These are the critical aspects of this job vacancy but you could add more if you have CAD experience (or are acquiring it) and by expressing your desire to be part of a progressive team. It would also pay to find out about the company in order to add that 'bit extra' that demonstrates initiative and genuine interest.

NEW BUSINESS DEVELOPMENT OFFICER
(Circa £20,000 p.a. Review Pending)

The purpose of this job is to establish an effective and developing programme to increase the awareness and motivation for young people to set up and maintain new business and/or become self-employed within Hertfordshire. You will also establish an administrator and vocational education and training group and implement its policies by working closely with a variety of organisations and assist in establishment of a career education programme.

Experience of supervisory or administrative posts involving successful innovative projects and experience of self-employment or working in a small company is advantageous. You must be able to deal with a wide range of people from MD to self-employed entrepreneur in a diverse range of public and private organisations. This is suitable for a "self-starter" who is looking for a challenging and rewarding position to enhance and develop career opportunities. A broad education to NVQ Level III or IV in business administration or related area is required.

Applications are particularly welcome from those residing within one hour's driving time. Please reply in confidence, enclosing a full C.V. and quoting the reference NBDO to: Jan Host, Human Resources Manager, Hertfordshire Training & Development Council, Eldon St. East, St. Albans, Herts AL4 2HA.

This is an 'in-depth' job notice. There is a lot of information and you need to work carefully through it to identify the key attributes they are seeking, and then relate these to your own experience.

- One word that appears often is "establish". Emphasis is also given to "implement", "innovative" and "self-starter". They probably consider attributes such as initiative, creativity, self-motivation and entrepreneurship to be *very* important, particularly in relation to developing programmes, training or education schemes.

- Just as significant is the need for excellent communication skills, both within groups and across broad sections of the community - young people, business people of all ages, bank managers, small retail shop owners, public sector organisations and so on.

- Although not essential, a definite bonus if you are able to provide evidence of past successes and competence in business administration.

- Provide evidence of desire for a challenging career and long-term career development.

- In summary, some key skills/attributes they appear to want include:

  - initiative
  - planning/management
  - creativity/innovative thinking
  - communication/liaison
  - co-ordination
  - self-motivation/drive/enthusiasm
  - track record
  - knowledge of/skills in group dynamics
  - long-term vision
  - administration

ASSISTANT CONSULTANT

Friendly, lively graduate, who enjoys dealing with people, to help us in the recruitment of lawyers. Previous office experience essential: telesales experience an advantage. C.V.s to John Smith, Smith & Partners, George Lane, Mildenhall, Suffolk IP27 6EY.

This job notice offers few clues. It is not explicit about how the person is to "help us in the recruitment of lawyers", nor does it define "office experience". Nevertheless, we must glean from it what we can.

- Personality is important, as denoted by the words "friendly", "lively" and "enjoys dealing with people". While this is not always easy to convey in a covering letter and C.V., you need to emphasise qualities such as compatibility, easy-going nature, involvement in social club activities, etc and provide evidence where possible (performance assessments, for instance).

- Communication skills need to be emphasised - reception, listening, dealing with complaints, empathy.

- Any experience in recruitment should be mentioned.

- Office experience - use of office equipment, office administrative systems, workload management, basic accounting. If you have a wide range of office skills it would pay to mention them all, since their requirements are unspecified and yet this feature of the job is essential.

- Obviously telesales experience should be emphasised if you have it.

RESEARCH ASSISTANT

£14,910 p.a.

Based in our headquarters, the person appointed will contribute to a new policy initiative to develop and promote community prisons and to other work in the Research Section, including resettlement needs of people leaving prison and international comparisons in criminal justice. The post will involve assisting with collation and analysis of information, with the drafting of papers for the Advisory and Policy Committees and with the organisation of conferences and seminars. The person appointed will need to have, or be able to acquire quickly, some knowledge of criminal justice, particularly the prison system, of research methods and basic computer skills. The work will require a well organised approach and will involve liaison with a wide variety of people, including people in other countries. Preference may be given to applicants who have some knowledge of another European language. This post is suitable for job-sharing.

For a description and application form, please contact Colin Jones, Research Section, Resettlement League, 142 Christchurch Road, London SW8 0PU. Telephone (071) 567 2300 ext 453. Applications should be received by 24 May 1992.

We aim to be an equal opportunities employer and to eliminate unfair discrimination against anyone in our selection process.

Your first action should be to obtain the job description and application form. From the notice we can see that the key skills to be emphasised and evidenced are:

- ability to work effectively in a team
- research skills and methods
- analytical
- written communication
- organisational - specifically conferences/seminars but also personal work habits
- effective communication/liaison across the community
- ability to be 'quick on the up-take' and/or possess technical knowledge required (i.e. criminal justice, prison system, computer skills, foreign language skills)

When you have identified the key attributes sought in a job notice, the next step is to construct the covering letter.

6 *The covering letter*

The C.V. must be accompanied by a covering letter, addressing the job for which you are applying. Remember that the covering letter is the *first* thing the employer will read. If it is unimpressive or poorly written the employer may not even bother to read the C.V. So it is important!

Layout

If you are unfamiliar with standard letter layout, here are some basic tips:

- Put your address and phone number either in the top right hand corner of the page or the top left. Make sure you include your telephone number - you need to be as accessible as possible.

- Date your letter. Put it on the same side as your address and telephone number.

- Always put to whom you are writing (the addressee), using their name and designation (Personnel Manager, General Manager etc.) if known, followed by the name and address of the organisation. This goes at the left hand margin, always.

- A couple of lines below that is the salutation, which is either Dear Sir or Dear Madam or Dear Sir/Madam (use the latter if unsure of person's gender). If, however, the advertisement has asked you to write to a particular person rather than the 'Personnel Manager', use their name in the salutation. This goes at the left margin.

- Use paragraphs at sensible intervals - it makes your letter easier to read.

- Sign off, 'Yours faithfully'. Note that when it's Dear Sir or Madam, Yours faithfully is used. When it's Dear Mr, Mrs, Ms Somebody, Yours sincerely is used. Put the sign-off to the right if your address above is on that side, otherwise it goes at the left margin.

- Your signature. Sign your name, using your usual signature, then neatly print/type your name in block letters underneath.

● Type or hand write? Employers' attitudes on this vary widely. My professional opinion is that a typed letter complements the typed C.V. Remember, it's not just a 'job application', it's a personal presentation package. But, *always* sign the letter by hand. Occasionally an advertisement will specify "in applicant's own handwriting". Obviously it would be foolish not to comply.

Content

Above all, be brief. Your covering letter should be no longer than one typed page.

It is important to answer two key questions: Why do you want the job? Why do you think you should get it? You could organise your letter like this:

Opening paragraph

If you are replying to an advertised position, you could use the following, stating where and when you saw the notice:

> *I am applying for the position of _____, as advertised in _____ on _____.*

or

> *Through the _____ magazine, _____ issue, I learned of your opening for a _____.*

If you have been independently researching companies, something like this might suffice:

> *I have been researching the local _____ industry to determine companies that are respected in the field and that provide career planning opportunities. _____ appears consistently as a top company.*

or

> *After researching the local _____ industry, I would like the opportunity to put my skills, _____ years of experience, and self-motivation to work for _____.*

Second paragraph

Having studied the job notice or job description, you will have identified the key skills and attributes the employer is seeking. Outline briefly your relevant experience, skills, qualifications and strengths and say in a positive way how these make you most suited to the position. Refer the reader to your attached C.V.

For example:

> *Over the past seven years I have successfully applied my knowledge of computer hardware and software to the competitive computer industry and have established an impressive track record. Notably, I attained the Branch Sales Award for six consecutive months. I notice "high achievement" is one area you stress as important in your advertisement. You will see that my attached Curriculum Vitae demonstrates a history of determination, motivation and a will to succeed.*

Third paragraph

Now you must say why you want the job. And the 'why' has to have an appeal or benefit for the reader. For example, you don't say you want the job because you're tired of being on the unemployment benefit or sick of being stuck at home. You want the job because of factors like challenge, variety, interest, the type of organisation (e.g. market leader, go-ahead), the product/service (what you like about it), the people (the desire to be part of their team), strong commitment to a particular relevant philosophy, and so on. Sounds like you're buttering them up doesn't it? Well you are, but there must be an underlying truth to it otherwise why bother applying? Clearly, if it's a job you're serious about, it would pay to do some homework. Find out as much as you can about the organisation, the industry, the vacancy. Talk to people, look at annual reports, promotional literature, policy statements, etc. If they see this depth of interest, they'll be interested. Useful phrases might include:

> *...I would welcome the opportunity to be part of a dynamic team...*

> *...I am keen to work in an environment where I can fully utilise my skills and experience to further both the organisation's goals and my own career aims...*

> *...The position offers the challenge, variety and stimulation I am seeking...*

> *...I am impressed with the image of _____ in the community and would feel privileged to be able to contribute...*

Fourth paragraph

This is the closure. Don't waffle. Don't use phrases like, "Thanking you in anticipation" or something equally dull. Finish by stating your availability for an interview and your willingness to provide further information. For example:

> *I look forward to discussing my background in more depth at an interview. Please contact me at any time at the above number.*

> *I would welcome the opportunity to meet you and discuss ways in which my skills and experience would benefit your organisation. Please contact me on _____ .*

> *I am very keen to meet you to discuss the requirements of this vacancy and my suitability for it. Please contact me on _____ for an interview at a time convenient to you.*

If you are 'cold-calling', i.e. initiating contact, you may want to state that you will contact them on a specific date to arrange a meeting.

7 Examples

Following are examples of job notices, covering letters, and C.V.s. Apart from the first one, the C.V.s have been abridged, with Education, Interests, etc omitted. They are all fictitious and any resemblance to a person is pure coincidence.

Example 1

> **BOOKSHOP ASSISTANT**
>
> We have a vacancy in our bookshop for a person who is self-motivated, can communicate well with the public, is interested in books and shows initiative.
>
> No formal qualifications are required but a relevant work history would be an advantage. Write to the Manager, A-Z Bookshop Ltd, 14 High Street, Stratford-upon-Avon. Applications close 14 March 1991.

23 Cloverley Close
Oxford
(Phone: (865) 513-4475)

25 February 1991

The Manager
A-Z Bookshop Ltd
14 High Street
Stratford-upon-Avon

Dear Sir/Madam

I am applying for the position of Bookshop Assistant, as advertised in the Globe newspaper on Saturday 23 February.

I have recently completed a 12 week training course on retail selling, which has equipped me with customer service, cash handling, telephone ordering, packaging and window dressing skills, all of which are relevant to the vacancy. The course also taught me to become self-motivated, confident in approaching people, and skilled at using my initiative to solve customer problems. I have always had a keen interest in books and currently read about 20 a year. I believe my skills, experience and enthusiasm make me particularly suited to this position. My attached Curriculum Vitae provides further details.

The A-Z Bookshop is well known and respected in Stratford, as highlighted in the recent book launching hosted in your store. When I have visited the bookshop, I have been delighted at the wide range of books available and have always found your staff most helpful. To be able to work in such an environment would provide the variety, interest and stimulation I am seeking in a job.

I am available at any time for an interview and would be happy to provide further information. Please contact me at the above number.

Yours faithfully

HELEN FRENCH (Ms)

CURRICULUM VITAE

NAME: Helen Ann French

ADDRESS: 23 Cloverley Close
                    Oxford

TELEPHONE: (865) 513-4475 (day and night)

DATE OF BIRTH: 15 January 1971 (20 years)

NATIONALITY: English

PERSONAL SKILLS & ABILITIES:

Training Course Experience (Course Certificate enclosed)

As a trainee on a 12 week Retail Selling Course, I have -

- learnt and demonstrated the keys to customer service - personal presentation, self-confidence, product knowledge, listening, empathy and courtesy.

- learnt and demonstrated the keys to selling - approach, evaluation, presentation, objections, closing.

- handled cash and am skilled in all retail calculations.

- become proficient in the operation, function and balancing of cash registers.

- learnt the principles of stock control.

- displayed stock in a well presented, attractive fashion.
- written sales tickets and participated in dressing a shop window for a competition between trainees.
- arranged stock replacement.
- demonstrated knowledge of security procedures.
- learnt authorisation procedures for cheques, credit cards and invoices.
- demonstrated a professional telephone manner.

Personal Service Experience

As a waitress, I have -

- dealt courteously with the public.
- kept food areas clean and tidy.
- listened carefully to instructions from both the public and bar management.
- handled complaints with patience and empathy.

School Experience

As a school student, I have -

- been on the school library committee, participating in decisions on book purchases.
- helped organise a school fete.
- delivered a speech to the entire school (600 students), as part of the Fifth Form Speech Competition.
- participated in school plays.
- worked with others on school projects.
- researched topics for assignments, involving library research and interviewing skills.

EMPLOYMENT HISTORY:

Oct - Dec 1990	Training Course on Retail Selling (12 weeks), A & B Training Providers, Oxford.
Jan 1990 - Sept 1990	Unemployed
1988 - Dec 1989	Waitress, Hong Kong Restaurant, Main Road, Oxford. Made redundant in December 1989 due to financial constraints on employer.

EDUCATION:

Secondary

1984 - 1987	St. Katherine's College, South Street, Swindon.
	G.C.S.E - English, Mathematics, Biology.
	Speech Prize - 3rd Form
	English Award - 5th Form.

Primary

1976 - 1983	Mt Pleasant Primary School, North Road, Swindon.
	Prize for Diligence - 5th year.
Other	Currently undertaking a correspondence course on bookkeeping.

INTERESTS:

Reading (Member of Doubleday Book Club)
Story-writing and story-telling (for children)
Music
Handcrafts - knitting, patchwork, tapestry
Walking/tramping
Dining out with friends.

REFERENCES:

A reference from Mr Lam, of the Hong Kong Restaurant, is attached.

A verbal reference can be obtained from Ms Peters (Principal Tutor), A & B Training Providers, on Oxford 688-2429.

Example 2

OFFICE ASSISTANT

Action for Health

- Part Time -

Action for Health is a community based health education service. We require a competent person to undertake office duties 20 hours per week including word processing (Microsoft Word or WordPerfect), filing, correspondence, minute-taking at monthly meetings, and other duties as required. Previous office experience essential. Reply Helen Crawford, Action for Health, 180B Hamlin Street, Harrogate, North Yorkshire NH6 2IP.

---

22 Rose Hill
Harrogate

Tel: 544-921

19 September 1992

Helen Crawford
Action for Health
180B Hamlin Street
HARROGATE NH6 2IP

Dear Ms Crawford

I wish to apply for the position of Office Assistant, Action for Health, as advertised in The Evening Post on 14 September.

Over the past six years I have gained experience in all facets of office procedures including word processing, filing, telephone-answering and reception, minute-taking (Pitman 2000, 100 wpm), basic accounting and more recently some basic desk-top publishing for newsletters. My attached C.V. provides details on my background.

In addition, I am also a mother of one child, and a volunteer Support and Development worker for handicapped children. These roles have endowed me with patience, sensitivity and empathy.

I strongly endorse the need for health education and would be an enthusiastic and supportive member of the Action for Health team.

Please contact me if you require further information. I look forward to meeting you.

Yours sincerely

Emma E Cranshaw

CURRICULUM VITAE

NAME: Emma Elizabeth CRANSHAW

ADDRESS: 22 Rose Hill
                  Harrogate

TELEPHONE: (214) 544-921

DATE OF BIRTH: 28 October 1960 (33 years)

HEALTH: Very good

DEPENDANTS: Child aged 7

PERSONAL SKILLS & ABILITIES

Office Experience

During six years of part-time secretarial/office experience (1978-1983), I developed the following skills:

- wordprocessing (am familiar with Wordstar, WordPerfect and Microsoft Word and recently completed refresher Polytechnic course - 1991).

- set up filing systems.

- reception and telephone answering.

- shorthand (100 wpm).

- handling customer complaints.

- maintenance of cashbook and payment of accounts.

Community Work

- IHC Support and Development Worker for 6 years (1987 to present) involving skills such as communication, patience, sensitivity and flexibility.

55886

- Playcentre committee member and worker with Stage 2 certificate. Skills developed include conflict resolution, relationships, group facilitation, fund raising.

Parenting (1986 to present)

In addition to those already stated under 'Community Work', I have developed the following skills:

- listening
- organising - kindergarten days/school events, etc which involved attending meetings, liaising with people in the community, meeting deadlines, co-ordination skills.
- participated in parent help at school.
- budgeted the family income.
- supported children's activities such as ballet, sports days, school plays.

EMPLOYMENT HISTORY (Paid)

1984 to present	Support & Development Worker, IHC, Harrogate (part-time/casual).
1978 - 1983	Typist/receptionist, Department of Labour, Harrogate (full-time).

Example 3

MINSELL JEWELLERY AGENT

We are a leading company in the importation of top-of-the-range silver and amber jewellery, our quality collections being distributed within the EEC, USA and Japan.

We are seeking an Agent for the UK who already has good connections with the most prestigious jewellers and stores with jewellery departments.

Experience, dynamism, motivation and a good track record in this field are essential. Minsell offers an attractive remuneration package. To apply, please write enclosing a full C.V. to: The Director-General, Swedish Chamber of Commerce, Knightsbridge House, Knightsbridge, London SW6 4RB by 14 October 1991.

---

45 Powis Lane
Willisden
LONDON WC2 4BH

Tel: (081) 578 2147

9 October 1991

The Director-General
Swedish Chamber of Commerce
Knightsbridge House
Knightsbridge
LONDON SW6 4RB

Dear Sir/Madam

RE: JOB NOTICE: MINSELL JEWELLERY AGENT

I am applying for the above position, which was advertised in The Observer on 6 October 1991.

I am well aware of Minsell's products, having been involved in selling jewellery and other lines for 10 years, and have always been impressed by the consistently high standard of craftsmanship. In particular, your *Oban* range appears to have achieved impressive market penetration since its release.

In the last five years I have been an agent for Crosswells here in the UK and have established stable links with most of Britain's reputable jewellery firms. You will see from my attached C.V. that I am a dedicated and motivated salesperson, who believes in nurturing clients for long term benefit.

I would welcome the opportunity to represent a company whose products are so well respected and am eager to meet the challenge of providing superior service to your clients.

I look forward to meeting you and talking more about how I could contribute to the Minsell team. Please contact me on the above number.

Yours faithfully

MARIA STANHOUSE

CURRICULUM VITAE

NAME:	Anna Maria STANHOUSE (known as Maria)
ADDRESS:	45 Powis Lane, Willisden, London WC2 4BH
TELEPHONE:	(081) 578 2147 (bus and pvt)
DATE OF BIRTH:	12 April 1963
MARITAL STATUS:	Married with no children
NATIONALITY:	British citizenship 1984 (Country of Origin: Italy)
HEALTH:	Excellent

PERSONAL STRENGTHS

self-motivation
dedication to work
client care
efficient sales technique
results-oriented
energetic and innovative
excellent personal presentation

PERSONAL STRENGTHS & ABILITIES

As a sales agent since 1982 (refer Employment History for details) I have developed the following specific skills.

Selling & Customer Relations

- effective sales technique based on an integration of personal study, personal confidence, training course material, and real-life experience. I know what works. Last year I won a Merit Award for Sales.

- a thorough knowledge of the UK jewellery market.

- on-going study of the market to keep abreast of changing needs (subscribe to Lithcombe's monthly magazine).

- excellent customer relations and rapport. A number of prestigious clients will deal only with me when purchasing from Crosswells.

- a thorough understanding of the retail system which enables me to empathise with my customers and provide quality service.

Business Management

- an organised and methodical approach to work. All customers and purchases are loaded onto a database which provides valuable sales information and assists in the formulation of sales plans.

- good follow-up after visits e.g. letters of thanks, and regular contact.

- undertake own basic accounting and office management tasks.

EMPLOYMENT HISTORY

| 1987 to present | Sales Agent for Crosswells Jewellery, London. Range includes jewellery and some accessories. Refer to sales performance report attached. |
| 1982 - 1986 | Sales Agent, Gemini, London. Range included cosmetics, perfume, jewellery and accessories. Reference attached. |

Example 4

Following a telephone enquiry to the Nursing Department at a local polytechnic, Janette Sanders was invited to submit her C.V. She had approached the polytechnic as part of her job research plan to see if they had any tutoring vacancies. There was no actual advertised vacancy.

Janette Sanders
45 Rowley Drive
Twickenham
London W6 9XR

Tel: (081) 752 3448

14 January 1992

Mrs C Roach
Director of Nursing
Nursing Department
Vector Polytechnic
175 College Heath Road
LONDON W11 5AH

Dear Celia

Further to our telephone conversation about possible tutoring vacancies in the Nursing Department, I am happy to enclose my Curriculum Vitae for your consideration.

You will recall we talked about the department's need for a community-based focus to some of its core courses. You will see that my experience in community based care is broad and pro-active. I believe this practical experience would greatly benefit students - afterall, a major principle of community-based health is empowering people to take responsibility for their own health care.

Over the 15 years I have been involved in health, there have been many opportunities to identify education needs and initiate programmes to meet them. For example, a physiotherapy service at Cheltenham Hospital, workshops for adult intellectually handicapped, establishment of various self-help groups. This skill is also something health students specialising in community-based health care need to develop.

I am keen to meet you and discuss my background and your department's needs further. I can offer real skills and experience to students in an enthusiastic and positive way.

I will telephone you on the 21st to arrange a convenient time. Thank you for the opportunity to present my Curriculum Vitae.

Yours sincerely

JANETTE SANDERS

CURRICULUM VITAE

NAME: Janette Ellen SANDERS

ADDRESS: 45 Rowley Drive, Twickenham, LONDON W6 9XR

TELEPHONE: (081) 752-3448

DATE OF BIRTH: 15 May 1951

MARITAL STATUS: Divorced

DEPENDANTS: None. Two grown children aged 18 and 21.

HEALTH: Excellent

PERSONAL QUALITIES
I WOULD BRING TO A TEACHING POSITION

Ability to work collaboratively
Sensitivity to cultural differences
Well developed communication skills
Proven ability to work well under pressure
Ability to be pro-active
Ability to prioritise tasks and
organise work demands effectively
Empathy and support
Enthusiasm for remaining professionally updated and
passing knowledge on

PERSONAL SKILLS & ABILITIES (1976 to present)

Teaching Experience

- planned and presented courses on parenting, ante-natal and post-natal education.

- co-ordinated programmes in primary/secondary schools, e.g. drug and alcohol, sexual health, pubertal change.

- conducted one-day seminars on pre-menstrual tension, menopause, women's sexuality, death and dying.

- taught stress management, family planning, healthy eating, and basic massage techniques to a wide variety of people, e.g. factory workers, students, business people, women's groups.

- contributed to various health education campaigns such as Keep Kids Safe, Sunsense, immunization and infectious diseases.

- readily addressed questions at seminars/workshops on whatever topic arose, e.g. diabetes, asthma, cot death, blood pressure, ageing, and so on.

- assisted other health professionals at health fairs, women's health days and adolescent days.

Community Health Initiatives

- researched and established:
    - a physiotherapy service at Cheltenham Hospital
    - adult workshops for intellectually handicapped
    - Cheltenham Family Health Counselling service

- established self-help groups:
    - diabetic
    - asthmatic
    - post-natal depression
    - migraine

- promoted and co-ordinated the establishment of a regional Child Protection Team.

- collaborated to make numerous submissions over the years to government, local bodies and service agencies on the social impact of legislative changes.

- organised and marketed a major fund-raising event for the establishment of a Community Centre.

SERVICE ON COMMUNITY COMMITTEES

1990 - present	Women's Health Group, Twickenham
1990 - present	West London Drug & Alcohol Committee
1990 - present	West London Community Focus Committee
1988 - 1989	Co-ordinator Cheltenham Care & Protection Resource Panel
1987 - 1988	Cheltenham Region Child Protection Team
1987 - 1989	Cheltenham Community Health Committee
1985 - 1988	Women & Family Emergency Housing Committee
1980 - 1989	Women's Health Group, Cheltenham

EMPLOYMENT HISTORY

1990 - present	Public Health Nurse, Twickenham (providing psychiatric, industrial, family health)
1986 - 1989	District Nurse, Cheltenham Public Hospital
1984 - 1985	Staff Sister, Cheltenham Public Hospital
1980 - 1983	Part-time nursing, Cheltenham, and raising family
1977 - 1979	Staff sister, Cheltenham Public Hospital, General Surgical Ward
1976	Staff Nurse, Staff Sister, Swindon Public Hospital

Note: Other headings which might be relevant in this example may include: Courses Attended, Papers Presented, Research Experience, Publications, Professional Memberships, Personal Philosophy, as well as the usual Education & Qualifications, Interests and References.

Example 5

BUILDER'S LABOURER

We require a labourer to assist on our construction sites. Labouring/apprentice carpentry experience essential. Must be reliable, hard-working, and able to work in a team. Good hourly rate offered. Apply outlining experience to Jim Brown, Brown Earthworks Ltd, 134 Downpipe Lane, Scunthorpe SN4 3BX.

2/53 Brook Lane
Scunthorpe

Tel: 284 326

26 August 1991

Mr Jim Brown
Brown Earthworks Ltd
134 Downpipe Lane
SCUNTHORPE SN4 3BX.

Dear Mr Brown

I am replying to your advertisement in the Evening Star on Saturday 22 August for a Builder's Labourer.

I have had three years' experience as an apprentice carpenter and am familiar with a wide range of equipment and techniques. You will see from the enclosed Curriculum Vitae and reference that I am a hard-working and reliable person who gets on well with workmates.

The reason for leaving my last employer was the expiry of my apprenticeship contract and the lack of permanent openings available within their firm. I am now keen to continue putting training into practice and to become proficient at the building trade.

I am available any time for an interview and look forward to hearing from you. My telephone number is 284 326.

Yours sincerely

SIMON STONE

CURRICULUM VITAE

NAME: Simon Arthur STONE

ADDRESS: 2/53 Brook Lane, Scunthorpe

TELEPHONE: 284 326

MARITAL STATUS: Single

DRIVERS LICENCE: Current, motor car, heavy truck

HEALTH: Good

PERSONAL SKILLS & ABILITIES

Carpentry

- used a wide range of carpentry tools
- have a ramset licence
- carried out foundation work
- assisted in constructing buildings
- steel tying and bending
- made pre-fabricated slabs
- roofing
- door hanging
- placing windows
- digging trenches
- used compacter, thumpers, diggers, high pressure jack hammers
- forklift driving
- set up scaffolding and bracing
- undertaken building calculations
- interior finishing work
- cleaning job sites

Other Labouring

- used hand slashers to clear scrub
- operated circular saw weed-eaters and chain-saws
- painted house roofs, exteriors and fences
- undertaken paving, brick and block laying, planting and weeding
- general exterior maintenance

School Experience

- elected to represent my class on School Council
- participated in school plays
- represented my school in:

      – swimming   – rugby
      – badminton   – triathlon

EMPLOYMENT HISTORY

June 1988 - June 1991 Apprentice Carpenter, Cromwell Construction
Company, Grimsby.

Jan 1988 - May 1988 Odd-jobs - gardening, mowing lawns, fixing
windows, etc

Example 6

SENIOR BENEFITS OFFICER

Applications are invited for the above post following the current
postholder's move to the South-West.

The person appointed will supervise the day-to-day running of the
Benefits Section which deals with Housing Benefits and Community
Charge Benefits.

Applicants should be suitably experienced. They should be well
motivated, have a pleasant manner, and able to work with little
supervision.

In return you will work in a pleasant modern office and will be paid a
salary up to £14,484 with access to a higher grade.

Apply sending full C.V. to Mary Carruthers, Personnel Section,
Nottingham District Council, 24 Oswald Inn Fields, Nottingham NH7
4EE. Applications close 17 September 1991.

29 Gilbert Road
Bloxham Heath
HUCKNALL NH11 4BE

Tel: 578 4123 (home)

529 3490 (work)

12 September 1991

Ms Mary Carruthers
Personnel Section
Nottingham District Council
24 Oswald Inn Fields

NOTTINGHAM NH7 4EE

Dear Ms Carruthers

Thank you for the opportunity to apply for the position of Senior Benefits Officer, as advertised in Friday's edition of the Reflector.

For the last five years I have applied many of the skills needed to be a Senior Benefits Officer within the role of Student Loans Officer, Northern Polytechnic. Good communication skills, motivation and organised work habits are important and I have developed these to an extent where I now feel ready to apply them to a new situation.

My enclosed Curriculum Vitae provides full details of my experience and qualifications and you will notice from the personal assessments attached that I am a dedicated worker with energy to meet new challenges. I would welcome the opportunity to apply that energy in your office.

Please contact me on the above number. I look forward to meeting you.

Yours sincerely

Christine Joy STEVENS

CURRICULUM VITAE

NAME: Christine Joy STEVENS

ADDRESS: 29 Gilbert Road, Bloxham Heath,
                  Hucknall NH11 4BE

TELEPHONE: 578 4123 (home)   529 3490 (work)

DATE OF BIRTH: 21 August 1965

HEALTH: Excellent

PERSONAL SKILLS & ABILITIES

Administration & Supervisory Experience

As a Student Loans Officer, Northern Polytechnic, Nottingham (1986 - present), I:

43

- supervise three staff: check arrears records, delegate tasks, initiated a new work schedule for staff, prepare personal staff assessments, ensure section targets are met.

- prepare monthly reports for Student Loans Committee on number of new loans, state of current loans, type of enquiries received, performance of office staff, etc. Report back to staff to keep them informed and motivated.

- interview students for loans - check applications; ensure budgets are realistic; analyse affordability; check creditworthiness; explain their commitment; communicate at their level.

- interview students who have loan repayments in arrears. Requires high degree of sensitivity and tact. Present choices for them and liaise with appropriate agencies.

- handle complaints with empathy and action.

- train staff on computer system.

- have basic accounting skills - cash checking - end-of-day balance, banking, petty cash control, cashiering, accounts, calculate payments rates as required.

- sound knowledge of computer applications - applications registration, database maintenance, word processing.

PERSONAL QUALITIES

communicate well with clients and workmates
reliable
conscientious
enjoy challenges

EMPLOYMENT HISTORY

1986 - present	Student Loans Officer, Northern Polytechnic, Nottingham. Initially clerical, now in charge of three staff.
1983 - 1985	Bank Teller/Junior Loans Officer, Bank of Scotland, Edinburgh.
1981 - 1982	Shop Assistant, Mitchell's Vegetable Store, High Street, Hucknall.

Example 7

ASSISTANT CHEF

We require an assistant chef for our busy restaurant. Training will be given but a basic knowledge of food preparation and presentation is essential. Must have energy, imagination and ability to work well with others and under pressure. Occasional relief waiting of tables. Hours are 5pm - 1am Tuesday to Saturday. Apply to Steve Barrett, Toad Hall, 31 Lincoln Row, Avebury, Wiltshire WL4 2PA.

---

28 Stanley Close
Calne
WILTSHIRE WL7 4EP

Tel: 678-9192

4 July 1992

Steve Barrett
Toad Hall
31 Lincoln Row
Avebury
WILTSHIRE WL4 2PA

Dear Mr Barrett

Toad Hall has a reputation for having wonderful food and a warm atmosphere. I have always found this to be so when dining there. Naturally, when I saw your advertisement for an Assistant Chef in the latest Wiltshire News I was excited at the possibility of being part of the Toad Hall team.

I have recently completed a cookery course which taught me the basics of cookery, food preparation and hygiene. But more than this, it introduced me to the *excitement* of food; the endless possibilities of dishes, flavours and presentation. I am now ready to put this new energy and imagination to work for Toad Hall.

My enclosed Curriculum Vitae details my background and you will see that I would come to you with some restaurant experience under my belt and am also used to working night-time hours.

Please contact me on 678-9192 to arrange an interview. I would also be happy to prepare a "test dish" for you to critique.

I look forward to hearing from you.

Yours sincerely

Mark Yeats

CURRICULUM VITAE

NAME: Mark Charles YEATS

ADDRESS: 28 Stanley Close, Calne, Wilts WL7 4EP

TELEPHONE: 678-9192

DATE OF BIRTH: 9 February 1969 (23 years)

NATIONALITY: British

MARITAL STATUS: Single

HEALTH: Excellent

DRIVERS LICENCE: Current (motor-car)

PERSONAL SKILLS & ABILITIES

Cooking Course (Course Certificate attached)

As a trainee on this course I have:

- gained knowledge of basic cookery and baking.
- a sound knowledge of kitchen safety.
- skills and experience in the use of most kitchen equipment.
- an understanding of food hygiene and the need for a balanced diet.
- knowledge of store-keeping and its importance.
- learned how to present food.
- learned restaurant service skills.

Personal Service Experience

As an employee in a restaurant and also a retail store, I have:

- learned to work as a member of a team.
- developed efficient work methods to cope with pressures.
- had practice in some aspects of cooking and use of kitchen equipment.
- experienced and enjoyed serving customers.

- dealt with customer complaints with patience and understanding.
- had some management training and been in charge of the kitchen and its staff while manager was absent.
- learned cashiering skills.
- ordered stock and carried out stock-taking.
- kept food areas clean and tidy.

Other Relevant Experience

- On a three week Survival course I learned the meaning of team work, the value of fitness, and gained confidence in myself.

- My job as a commercial cleaner taught me to work methodically and maintain standards.

- In my job at Ashcroft Meats I developed knife handling skills and learned the importance of hygiene and how to handle meat.

EMPLOYMENT HISTORY

Feb 1992 - June 1992	Cooking Course on Basic Cookery and Restaurant Service - VGF Ltd, trainers in food industry personnel, Swindon.
Apr 1991 - Feb 1992	Waiter, The Crock Pot, Calne. Left to undertake cookery course.
Dec 1990 - Mar 1991	Unemployed. Undertook Survival course during this time.
Jan 1989 - Dec 1990	Overseas travel - working holiday in Australia and New Zealand. Bar work, restaurants and labouring.
Nov 1987 - Dec 1988	Commercial cleaner, Enterprise Cleaning Company, Devizes. Left to travel overseas.
Jan 1986 - Oct 1987	Junior butcher, Ashcroft Meats, Swindon - temporary position.
July 1985 - Dec 1985	Assistant, McDonalds Family Restaurant. Left after being uninspired.
Feb 1984 - June 1985	Temporary positions - supervised children at a baby clinic; delivered mail.

8 Presentation

About 80% of your chance for an interview rests on good presentation. No matter how much effort has gone into identifying skills and all other relevant information, if you fail to attract sufficient interest in that first vital instance, the opportunity is lost.

There are endless possibilities for presenting your information and the lengths you go to will reflect your interest in that job.

Everyone's idea of good presentation differs but here are some basic guidelines which will help to set your application apart:

- All sheets of paper submitted should be standard A4 size (i.e. 210mm x 300mm). Scrawled hand writing on small light-weight letter writing paper is out! Not only will it get lost but it is also a poor competitor with more professional presentations.

- Your C.V. should be presented in a folder. There is a multitude available but one type which impresses me is the plastic folder with transparent envelopes in which all the pages are placed. Not only does this keep everything immaculate, but it also makes it easy for the reader to flip pages back and forth. If the idea of 'giving' one of these folders away seems too costly, it is acceptable to request its return if your application is not successful (preferably uplift it yourself if the position was local). There is an instance where this type of folder may not be appropriate. Some Government positions are considered by panels, which requires the C.V. to be photocopied several times. This is easier if the C.V. is stapled and not in a plastic folder. It also minimises the risk of pages being lost or put in the incorrect order. If you are unsure which would be appropriate, ring and ask.

- You may wish to enclose a photograph of yourself. It adds a human touch. Better still, can you include an 'action' photo? For example, for a teaching position, a photo of you teaching a class. It adds impact! If you do use a photograph, make sure you look friendly and approachable.

- Can you make your C.V. more innovative? For example, can you use photographs instead of words to show achievements? It cuts down on words and gives the reader visual relief. What about a title page - large lettering with a border around the page:

CURRICULUM VITAE (centred) FOR (centred) YOUR NAME (centred)? Can you include actual pieces of work (e.g. fabric for a weaver), newspaper clippings, and so on. Be careful not to get too carried away and make sure it's relevant!

- You may want to use coloured paper - it will make your application stand out. Use soft pastel shades rather than bold colours.

- If possible, have your C.V. typed onto a wordprocessor. Your C.V. is a flexible document, which means it will be altered many times throughout your life. I like the idea of having a 'foundation C.V.', one which has all your identified (and grouped) skills. Each time you apply for a job, you copy this document and tailor it to the job. That way, you've always got the 'original' C.V. on hand. A wordprocessor makes this task easy. Another possibility is to have it desktop published (typesetting by computer), which gives you a wonderful variety of type styles and sizes.

Finally

- have someone check over your C.V. and covering letter to make sure they make sense and are free of errors.

- always keep copies of everything you send.

- take a copy of your C.V. and covering letter to the interview. Make sure you can expand or explain what is written.

PART II

Facing the interview

9 Doing your homework

We often work ourselves into a terrible state over an interview. Our
stomachs churn, hands sweat, breathing becomes shallow, and our
nails are bitten to the quick. There will always be an element of
nervousness, but one thing is sure: the key to successful interviews is
to diminish the element of surprise through thorough preparation and
understanding what the employer wants.

I believe that if you receive positive feedback about your
'performance', even though you may not have won the job, then the
interview was to some degree successful. It is important not to be
discouraged by missing a job, and to recognise that poor interviewer
skills are as common as poor interviewee skills. In these days of high
unemployment it is a real achievement to be granted an interview, and
there has often been much investment of time and energy to get there.

For the employer, there has been a great deal of thought invested in
whether to hire someone at all, and if so, what the job will be, what
skills and attributes the employee will need to possess, and all the
associated areas of job creation and definition.

One of the first points of contact between the employer and applicant
is the Job Description (sometimes called a Job Specification). It is
essential to obtain one if available. In most instances a Job Description
will be provided for the vacancy.

What can I learn from a job description?

A Job Description is just that; a description of the job that is vacant.
As with C.V.s, they vary widely but generally contain:

POSITION: Job title, e.g. Administration Officer.

SALARY: Often a range, e.g."£11,500 -£14,000 depending on
experience and qualifications".

DEPARTMENT/DIVISION/SECTION: Only relevant for medium to
large size organisations.

LOCATION: Suburb, town or city.

REPORTING TO: Title of person, e.g. Operations Manager.

DESCRIPTION: Brief overview of the main responsibilities of the position. May include notes on shift-work, stand-by, or other specific requirements.

OBJECTIVES: The reason for the vacancy's existence, e.g. "to provide full secretarial support to management". There may be several objectives for a vacancy - this will depend on its complexity.

KEY TASKS (OR DUTIES): A list of what the position involves. This is a good resource from which to ask questions at the interview.

RESPONSIBILITIES: Who the person is responsible to and who (if any) they have responsibility for, e.g. "for three office clerical staff".

KEY RESULT AREAS (OR PERFORMANCE INDICATORS): What will need to happen if the duties are to be carried out successfully, e.g. "the duties are being carried out successfully when (a) the plant is well maintained and operating efficiently; (b) work stations are clean and tidy; (c) staffing requirements are met.

PERSON SPECIFICATION: A list of the attributes sought for the position. It may be a fuller version of what appeared in the newspaper, e.g. "the person will have had at least five years' experience in welding, TCB qualifications, be able to work in a team, physically fit ...".

CONDITIONS OF APPOINTMENT: Annual and sick leave entitlements, superannuation, other benefits and conditions.

Occasionally, additional information is supplied which may include an overview of the department/company/industry, a budget for the department, lines of communication and working relationships within the organisation.

The job description, and any additional information, will give you a clearer understanding of the position, raise questions about it, and will be an important source for anticipating questions you may be asked.

Other sources of information

Your C.V.

If you've followed the guidelines set down in *Part I*, you will have submitted a well prepared and effective document to represent you on your behalf. This will go a long way towards ensuring you a place on the shortlist. But don't forget about your C.V. yet. It is an important resource in preparing you for the interview.

Go carefully through your C.V. to make sure you know what's in it. Feel confident that you could expand on what you have written and that you are sure of your strengths and aware of your limitations. Give thought to how you would overcome your limitations. For example, "Although I am reluctant to use computers, I have enrolled in a night class for beginners". "I sometimes take a long time to make a decision but I believe it is necessary to gather the facts first and also, I now give myself 'decision deadlines'." Don't over-focus on limitations and certainly don't state more than two. You could respond to this question with "The only limitations I have are those I place on myself, and I work hard to avoid doing that".

Take the C.V. with you to the interview.

Positive thinking

Write down the most positive aspects of your experience and qualifications. Go through each job or life event in your past and seek out the positive things - pats on the back, awards and recognition, times when you felt successful and confident (*see* Chapter 11: *What are employers looking for?* for more on this).

Information about the organisation

Pick up whatever information you can about the organisation through brochures and the like which explain their products/services, through talking to people who have been in contact with them, from annual reports, suppliers, past employees if known, and if appropriate, from the person in the front office/reception area. In some situations you may be able to get valuable information from the receptionist about what it's like to work in the organisation and you might be able to find out why the vacancy exists.

Looking through literature about the organisation can give you a feel for what business they are in ('business' including non-profit and community organisations). It is important to go to the interview with some understanding of the 'larger picture', that is, why the organisation exists, what it is trying to achieve (in a broad sense), and its history - how well established it is.

As well as equipping you well for the interview, this type of 'homework' or research will help to answer one of the most important questions you will be asked at the interview: why do you want the job?

We will look at questions later but it would be worthwhile at this preparation stage to actually *write down* your reasons for wanting the job. Remember the rule from your C.V. preparation: write for the reader. Your reasons must have an appeal in them for the employer - he/she must feel that hiring you would enhance the organisation and help it achieve its goals. Now think about how the job will enhance *your* life. How will it contribute to your happiness and career expectations? For example, it will use your analytical and problem-solving skills, the organisation is structured in a way that enhances your workstyle, you like the location, and so on.

Make sure you know when you would be available to start and try to be flexible about this if possible. Also make sure you have let your referees know about the job and that they understand what the employer is looking for.

In reality, this whole section is about 'doing your homework' because you need to think about all aspects of the position and interview beforehand. Homework is always a lot of work but let me ask you a question you will come across again in this book: how much do you want the job? Remember, for all the trouble you *don't* go to, you can guarantee someone else will.

Homework

Job Description

– helps you:

- **understand the job being offered**
- **anticipate questions you may be asked**
- **raise questions you need to ask**

– may include:

Position	**Reporting to**	**Responsibilities**
Salary	**Description**	**Key result areas**
Department	**Objectives**	**Person specification**
Location	**Key tasks**	**Conditions**

Other sources of information:

- **Your C.V.**
- **Positive thinking**

- Information about the organisation

  - brochures
  - annual reports
  - past employees

  - talking to their clients
  - suppliers
  - present employees

- Why do you want the job?

10 How is shortlisting done?

By being aware of the shortlisting process, applicants will gain some understanding of what is important to employers and how they reach decisions. It may be, for instance, that while an employer is satisfied with your written application, they may wish to check out some areas of personality or character at an interview. As a result, most of the questions asked may cover things *not* included in your application and based instead on referees' reports.

Various factors contribute to the shortlisting process. Firstly, and perhaps most obviously, the application and person's C.V. are the means by which the employer can judge potential suitability. They are looking for your experience, skills, qualifications. But they cannot do this in a vacuum. They will usually have some kind of checklist, often known as a person specification, and this will include factors critical to this position (known, not surprisingly, as 'critical factors'). Your application will be considered in light of the person specification and the critical factors.

As mentioned in Chapter 9: *Doing Your Homework*, a person specification details the attributes sought for the position, e.g. at least 5 years' relevant experience; has own car and clean licence; excellent telephone manner; non-smoker; excellent written and verbal skills. Those given the greatest weighting are the critical factors.

A method often used by employers to assist shortlisting, particularly if there are many applicants, is a recruitment grid where each applicant is considered under each category in the person specification. The shortlist will usually comprise six or fewer candidates.

Here's an example of how shortlisting might be achieved.

Vacancy: Typist

Key tasks: Wordprocessing (Microsoft Word or WordPerfect), filing, data inputing, telephone answering, other duties as required.

Person specification: High degree of accuracy and good speed (minimum of TCB GII), pleasant manner, good standard of English, at least 3 years' relevant experience, good numerical skills, drivers' licence;

Critical factors: Accuracy, speed, pleasant manner, good standard of English.

Recruitment grid:

Applicant	Accuracy	Speed	Pleasant	Good	Quality of manner*	Quality of English*	Quality of Application*
A	X	√	√	X	4		
B	√	√	√	√	2		
C	√	?	√	√	1		
D	√	√	√	√	2		
E	√	√	X	X	3		
F	√	√	√	√	1		
G	X	X	√	X	5		
H	√	√	√	X	4		
I	√	?	?	√	2		
J	√	√	√	√	2		
K	?	X	√	X	3		
L	√	?	√	√	1		
M	√	X	√	√	3		

*1 = Excellent   5 = Very Poor

Shortlist: From the grid, applicants B, C, D, F, J and L have the most number of desired characteristics. These will most likely be the shortlisted applicants, or fewer if fewer than six are required. In reality, there may be more than four critical factors.

Also worthy of note is the role that referees may play in shortlisting. In the above example, a 'pleasant manner' cannot be detected from a written application, so referees may be contacted for this information. They may be used as a matter of course; they may be used when the shortlist needs to be shorter but a decision cannot be made from the grid; or they may be used after an initial interview when a second shortlisting process may occur.

Other factors that may influence how shortlisting is achieved include equal employment opportunities legislation and perhaps the employer's personal preferences or perceptions, such as being keen on people who have demonstrated active community involvement or 'outside' interests, or who show they may possess the potential to contribute more than the requirements of the vacancy.

Shortlisting

- Helps you understand what's important to employers.

- Achieved by means of:
    - C.V./Application
    - Referees' comments
    - Person specification and critical factors - recruitment grid
    - Equal employment opportunities legislation.

C

11 *What are employers looking for?*

There are some attributes (characteristic qualities) that employers are most keen to see in applicants. Three important ones are:

- Communication skills
- Personal presentation
- Self-motivation

Communication skills

Part of the interviewer's perception of your ability to communicate will have already been formed by your written application. The test now will be to see how well you communicate verbally. Both what you say and how you say it will be important.

You may feel frustrated at having to repeat what you have taken pains to point out in your C.V. Remember, whether they've read your C.V. or only given it a cursory glance, they want to hear you talk. Look at it as another opportunity to sell yourself, only this time verbally rather than on paper.

If you do not communicate well verbally, it will be very important to practise in the mock interviews (*see* Chapter 15: *What can I expect to be asked?*) and to have stock answers prepared for what will probably be asked. There is no doubt that verbal competence is closely allied to confidence, and the more you practise, the more confident you will feel.

How confident are you of your skills and ability to do the job? How can you become confident? A person lacking confidence will:

- not smile
- not look you in the eye
- often look down at their feet
- appear uncomfortable
- be non-communicative

Is this you? You will need to do some serious pep-talking with yourself before you reach the interview.

First of all, re-read your C.V. to remind yourself of the skills and abilities you have. They are *valuable* and you *own* them. Then think about your work and/or school experience and write down all the positive and enjoyable things you can recall. Sit there until you have something written down:

● Got a good comment ("well researched and written") on an assignment to do with ...

● Did really well at the school sports day - school hero for a week!

● Solved a sticky administration problem in my last job and was congratulated by the boss for it.

● Felt great when I got an encore in the school play.

● Felt a real sense of achievement when I completed ...

● Really enjoy being able to solve customers' problems.

You see? You *have* done things of value and importance. And you are valued by others. What you need to do now is write that list out on a small card, carry it with you, and when you get the chance, read it as many times as you can during the day. Extend it. Include some of the skills from your C.V. if you wish. This is a method called 'affirmation' and there are many books available on such positive thinking techniques - ask at your local library.

And if you think this is a waste of time, try this: dissect your day so that every half-hour you stop and analyse how many negative thoughts and/or self-put-downs you have made in the previous half-hour (be honest!). Write them down. I'm sure many of us would have a long list by the end of the day, some longer than others. Often, this has been going on all our lives. Just imagine the effect of this on our self-esteem and confidence. Now imagine replacing those negative thoughts with positive ones. You have to do it deliberately and regularly because there are habits of a life-time to break. This is where affirmations come in. Every problem is now an opportunity for growth. Every situation of fear an opportunity for courage. Every moment of doubt a chance to reaffirm your self-worth and stride ahead.

Could you bring yourself to say some positive things about yourself? Try these:

● *I, (your name), have real personal confidence - I'll make it!*

- *I, (name), am very successful in all that I do. Success comes easily to me. I achieve what I desire.*

- *I, _____, am the equal of the best of people and truly am capable of great accomplishments.*

- *I, _____, can do anything I set my mind to because I have the utmost confidence in my abilities.*

- *I, _____, know I can do what I have to do, and I have to do what I set out to do.*

- *Every day in every way I'm getting better and better.*

It's hard to say them to begin with, especially aloud. That's because many of us are so unaccustomed to thinking and talking positively about ourselves. Try it. Write these out on another card and say them along with the first group. Add other ones that you may need, e.g. if you want to speak better, write an affirmation like "I, _____, am an excellent speaker. I speak clearly and concisely, and am understood by those listening." This will then become a *goal*, as will all the others, and will keep reminding you to practise speaking clearly and concisely. Eventually, you will achieve it. Remember, there are no limitations except those you place on yourself. Making realistic and achievable goals, affirming them constantly until achieved, and visualising the success (e.g. picturing yourself talking well, with everyone attentive and impressed) is a major step towards achievement and self-fulfilment.

How does this relate to the interview? In every way! You cannot communicate effectively if you have a negative attitude.

Personal presentation

This comes up time and again. How you present yourself matters. I'm talking about grooming (tidy and clean clothes, hair, hands, fingernails etc.), manner (pleasantness and personality), and poise (how well you carry yourself - see Body Language in the next chapter).

Your mode of dress should depend on the job and be influenced by the type of organisation. Dress for the part - how would the person who got the job be expected to dress? How formally will the interviewers be likely to dress? Fit into the model they have of the job, their organisation/staff.

How far should we go? Actually clean the heels of our shoes? Yes!
And fingernails. Iron a shirt/blouse, dryclean the suit, get a haircut or
make sure your hair is tidy. The lot! How much do you want the job?

Self-motivation

Equals enthusiasm. If you want the job, and know why, it's not
difficult to show it. Sometimes enthusiasm (so long as it's not
overdone) can make you 'sparkle'. There's a certain exuberance about
you, and if you follow this through by asking intelligent questions, it
can leave a very favourable impression in the interviewer's mind and,
importantly, help them to remember you when they come to make their
final choice.

You may also be able to point to occasions in the past where
self-motivation was evident. For example - night classes in typing that
led to achieving qualifications, a correspondence course to acquire
needed skills, and so on. Anything that shows you were motivated to
achieve something.

There are other important attributes too. Tick how many you believe
you have:

☐ Compatibility	☐ Good/relevant qualifications or education
☐ Pleasant personality	☐ Adaptability/flexibility
☐ The skills and knowledge required	☐ The potential to develop
☐ Honesty	☐ Initiative
☐ Problem-solving ability	☐ 'People' skills
☐ A stable work history	☐ Reliability
☐ Good health	☐ Career goals/aspirations
☐ Stress management skills	☐ Time management skills
☐ Professional attitude	☐ Confidence
☐ Empathy/understanding of customer service	☐ Self-discipline
☐ Loyalty	☐ Outside interests/community involvement
☐ Leadership qualities	☐ Level of preparedness for interview

Use the affirmations/visualisation method for any you want to acquire!

Attributes sought

- **Communication skills**

    - confidence
    - affirmations
    - practice

- **Personal presentation**

    - grooming
    - manner
    - poise

- **Self-motivation**

    - enthusiasm
    - evidence

- **Other attributes as detailed**

12 First things first

Focusing

Whether it's going to the dentist, having a job interview, sitting an exam, or some other daunting prospect, we often react with a "Let's pretend it's not happening" attitude. We carry on as normal, not preparing, not organising, and not 'psyching' ourselves for the event. All this does is disadvantage us.

Focusing is about facing up to the event, in this case the interview. It means knowing where the venue is, how you're going to get there, what time you have to leave home or work, and careful preparation the night before - making sure clothes and shoes are ready, your C.V. and other documents (such as the job description and questions you have noted to ask) are together, and going over your interview strategy. Visualise yourself going into the room greeting the interviewer, sitting, smiling, and answering the questions you anticipate will be asked. Then, put it out of your mind and get a good night's sleep.

Concentrating your mind will enhance your performance.

First impressions

Did you know that most employers have drawn conclusions about you within the first few minutes of meeting you? In the rest of the interview, they subconsciously seek to justify that impression. Unfortunately this is also the time when you are likely to be most nervous.

As with your C.V., you've only got one chance. As one employer once said: "You don't get a second chance to make a first impression".

What factors make a favourable first impression? Overwhelmingly, personal presentation matters. That is, appropriate, tidy and clean clothes, tidy and clean hair and appearance. Closely related to this is your manner - how you come across, your attitude, personality.

- Other important factors include
- confidence and assertiveness
- preparation for the interview

- communication skills (also critical throughout the entire interview, not just initially)
- enthusiasm for the position
- punctuality
- eye contact
- impressive application/C.V.

Body Language

Here are some important tips to retain control of your body in the interview. As Rowan Atkinson once said, "My body is my tool".

Pre-interview nerves

- Sit comfortably, close your eyes and breathe deeply and slowly for a minute - in through the nose, out through the mouth. Do this again just prior to going into the interview room.

- Walk for about 10-15 minutes before the interview.

- Slowly rotate your neck, then from side-to-side and up-and-down, to help release built-up tension.

- Make sure you go to the toilet before the interview.

- Buy some *Rescue Remedy* (bach flowers) from the chemist or homeopath. This is a homeopathic remedy for trauma and is a completely natural, chemical-free potion which will help you relax.

- Check and double check the venue, address, day, date, time and get there in plenty of time!

At the interview

- Greet the interviewer, or each panel member if this system is used, with a handshake and smile, looking them directly in the eye. If the panel is large in number or there is a physical barrier, such as a board table, shaking each person's hand may not be feasible. In that case, smile, nod and look at each person as they are being introduced to you. Try to remember names, though with a panel this may be difficult.

- Sit comfortably in the chair. The best way to sit in a chair is to place your bottom as far back on the seat as possible. This will keep your back straight and your position comfortable. Place your hands in your lap - don't wring them! Place your legs together, not crossed.

- Look the interviewer directly in the eye when they speak to you, or you to them. Look away when you are thinking of your response but guard against looking in one particular place, for example, looking repeatedly at the ceiling for inspiration. After a while you'll find everyone looking up there to see what's so interesting.

- Don't trip over your lip. Pause to think before you answer and talk slowly if you think you are in danger of gabbling. This is particularly important if you know the answer well or feel very confident about how to respond. So take a deep, imperceptible breath before answering. And, importantly, stop when you have said all you want to say. Let the interviewer pick up the silence.

- Smile when appropriate but don't overdo it. Just be yourself. If you're reasonably relaxed, smiling will come naturally. An opportunity for humour may arise, but not often. Watch the 'boundaries' of appropriateness.

- On leaving, smile, nod and thank the interviewer(s). It is not necessary to shake hands again. Watch at this point that your relief that the interview is over doesn't spill-over into some kind of inappropriate gesture or remark such as "Phew, I'm glad that's over" or "Did you say you knew so-and-so? I know them too. How come you know them...?" Just simply smile, thank, and leave.

First things first

- Focusing:
  - **Where is the venue?**
  - **How will you get there?**
  - **What time will you leave for the interview?**
  - **Night before -**

    clothes and shoes
    documents
    interview strategy

visualisation
early night

● First Impressions:

- One chance
- Personal presentation
- Manner/attitude/personality
- Confidence, and other factors - *see* previous chapter

● Body Language:

- Pre-interview -

    breathe deeply
    walk around beforehand
    neck exercises
    go to the toilet
    Rescue Remedy
    be punctual

- At the interview -

    greet with handshake, smile, eye contact
    sit comfortably, hands in lap, legs uncrossed
    eye contact, look away to think
    pause before responding, stop when finished
    speak up and clearly
    smile, watch humour
    leave: smile, nod, thank, go

13 What form will the interview take?

Formal interviews

Most interviews follow a relatively formal format where set questions are asked in a particular order by designated people (if a panel is used). They are generally taken by a person, or people, in middle or senior management, in a specified room, at set times.

In many cases a panel of interviewers is used for the "formal" interview. A "panel" is simply anywhere from 2 to 10 or more people (most often 2-6) who have an interest in the vacancy, either directly or indirectly. It is a means by which a joint decision on whom to employ can be made and since the vacancy can hardly be likely to affect only one person, this seems a sensible way of appointing.

The composition and operation of panels varies but some characteristics seem to be shared. The pre-interview planning usually involves the panel meeting to decide a number of factors. These may include reviewing the job description and person specification, the establishment of critical factors if not already done, reviewing and checking applicants, then shortlisting.

They will then set the questions, decide who asks what, agree the format and procedures for the interview (e.g. length, how recording is to be done, whether support people need to be invited etc.), and contact the shortlisted applicants to arrange a time.

Sex ratio is now an important consideration and although it may vary, it appears that the relevance of women's perspectives in hiring staff is at last being recognised. A sex ratio requirement is less evident among private enterprise than among public sector organisations.

Mostly, the question-asking will be shared, as each panel member asks questions specific to their area of expertise or interest.

Informal interviews

In an informal interview the atmosphere is more relaxed and the contact is one-to-one. The questions, too, may be less structured or job-related and tend to be open-ended, designed to assess personality, personal objectives, and communication skills. Usually, they are taken by non-executive staff and can be used for support staff, casual, part-time, and low-skilled vacancies.

Pre-interview briefings

Most employers do not fully brief applicants on what to expect. Some will provide a brief outline but mostly you will find out once you are there.

However, there is the slightest hint of a trend toward letting candidates know who will be on the panel, how long the interview will be and how it will operate.

Number of interviews

Don't be surprised if you end up having two interviews. Often the first one is a kind of shortlisting process with the second one being more in-depth for those shortlisted. Sometimes a second interview is held by a different interviewer who may be someone from senior management or another associated division or department.

Whether or not a second interview is held can also depend on the technical nature and/or the seniority of the position. In these cases the second interview will most often deal with the applicant's detailed knowledge.

A second interview might be necessary if applicants ranked equally in the first interview or some final confirmation or clarification is required. This will be the "decider".

A second interview might also be held if the interviewers have strong feelings about the unreliability of first impressions.

An applicant might be required to make a presentation at a second interview - e.g. for sales positions.

Support person

Can I bring someone with me? Most of the time supporters are not invited. However, if asked, some employers may be open to this suggestion and in some areas, particularly the public sector, it is common practice to make this option available for those who want it.

The supporter's role is generally that of a verbal referee for the applicant, providing evidence of their experience, skills and qualities.

This is often used for those ethnic groups for whom it is inappropriate to talk of one's own achievements and abilities.

The support person may also assist with interpreting questions, or may be a parent if the applicant is young, or may be present to help an applicant who has a disability.

In many cases the purpose of the supporter will be defined by the applicant.

Sometimes there may be some control on when the person may speak. For example, they may be asked to provide supporting comments at the end of, or at some other appropriate time during the interview.

Format

● **Interviews are mostly formal, i.e.:**

 – **Set questions**
 – **A panel of interviewers**
 – **Panel comprises middle-senior management, depending on status of vacancy**
 – **Usually between 2 and 6 people on the panel**
 – **More likely to be panel of mixed sex in public organisations**
 – **Question-asking shared by panel members**

● **Pre-interview planning by panel may involve:**

 – **A review of the job description and person specification**
 – **Setting of critical factors, if not already done**
 – **Review and check applicants**
 – **Shortlist applicants**
 – **Set questions and decide who asks what**
 – **Agree format and procedure**
 – **Contact shortlisted applicants**

● **Some interviews are informal and usually:**

 – **Are taken by one person (often non-executive)**
 – **Have a relaxed atmosphere**
 – **Contain open-ended, non-structured questions**

- A second interview might be required to:

    - Interview shortlisted applicants in-depth
    - Enable top management or another divisional manager to screen applicants
    - Look more deeply into technical details
    - Clarify points/confirm decision
    - Get a clearer picture of the 'real' you
    - Enable applicants to undergo a practical test, e.g. a sales presentation.

- Supporters:

    - Not usually invited
    - More common in the public sector
    - Often act as verbal referees
    - May attend to interpret questions
    - May attend to accompany a young applicant
    - May assist a disabled applicant

14 *How the interviewer might put you at ease*

Your nervousness prior to an interview is only natural, and interviewers are only human. They have various strategies designed to put you at ease. Not all work, of course, but this may be due as much to the interviewer's shortcomings as to your own acute tension.

The most common strategy to relax you is a warm and friendly welcome and a preliminary chit-chat unassociated with the job, organisation or interview. It might cover such innocuous topics as the weather, how you travelled to the interview, whether you watched the game last night, and so on. Sometimes, you may be given a tour of the department or organisation. This may be before or after the interview.

Also important is the interview room. Some employers (we hope most) will provide comfortable chairs and surroundings. This doesn't mean a sofa but seating that is both comfortable and arranged non-threateningly, and in a room that is appropriate, preferably without a desk and with instead a low coffee table between you and the interviewer(s).

Describing the format of the interview you are about to undergo is another tactic used to settle you and build rapport. Knowing how the time is to be spent will help to make you feel more comfortable. You will be introduced to panel members, if this type of interview is used - another ice-breaker.

Easing you gently in, the next move will be to start with the 'easy' questions which might include confirmation of some aspects of your C.V. such as address, phone number, etc.

The interviewer will probably then describe the vacancy and the organisation. So far, you've done very little talking and your understanding of the position and the organisation is probably expanding.

If they have done a good job of putting you at ease and setting up a 'safe' environment in which you can express yourself, you will feel empowered to answer any difficult questions confidently.

What if the interviewer doesn't put you at ease? As the power is not in your hands, there is little you can do. However, if you feel something is wrong, and you can think of an appropriate way of dealing with it, go ahead. For example, moving your chair to avoid glare, asking for water if your mouth is dry, asking questions for clarification, asking for feedback if the interviewer is sitting impassively, trying humour to cover a potentially embarrassing situation, and so on.

Putting you at ease

- Warm and friendly welcome
- Chit-chat
- Tour around
- Comfortable surroundings and non-threatening
- Describe interview format
- Introductions
- 'Easy' questions at the beginning
- Description of vacancy/organisation.
- If they don't put you at ease, could you:
- Shift chair?
- Ask for feedback?
- Ask for clarification?
- Use humour?

15 What can I expect to be asked?

Questions will always depend on the position being advertised but there are some which have become quite common to the interview situation.

Why do you want the job?

It is important to have clearly defined why you have applied for the position. Employers are keen to know where you see yourself heading, whether you would be likely to stay with the organisation, how enthusiastic you are and why, where your motivations lie, and what an asset you would be to the organisation. On the other hand, nothing turns employers off more than the indication that dollars or relief from boredom, or similar self-centred reasons, are why you have applied.

Some reasons for applying for a job might include:

- challenge and stimulation
- desire to be part of a team
- desire to be part of an organisation that has an impressive or proven track record
- desire to utilise skills, express self, fulfil needs of clients and self
- desire to grow and utilise potential
- sounds interesting and full of variety
- organisation has a sound reputation in the community
- organisation is go-ahead/pro-active

This is an opportunity to use some of the information uncovered when you did your 'homework' on the organisation.

Where do you see yourself in five years' time?

Here the interviewer wants to find out your goal-setting ability, your motivations and your commitment to success. A relatively general response would do, e.g. "I would like to be a key member of the sales team, having built up a solid client base and a proven sales track record...."

Outline your experience or tell us about yourself

The interviewer wants to flesh out the relevant experience.

Focus on the word 'relevant' and go back through previous jobs to extract the skills, training, responsibility, interests, appropriate personal characteristics, etc that are relevant.

Why are you thinking of leaving your present job?

or Why did you leave your last job?

Some reasons might include - lack of challenge or stimulation, didn't fully utilise acquired skills, redundancy, temporary or part-time, too much travelling, etc. If you were fired or asked to leave, try to put it in a positive way. Don't say "I got into an argument with the boss", rather "the boss and I had conflicting personalities" or similar, and add that usually you get on well with people. Emphasise your maturity or that you have changed your attitude.

What are your strengths?

Pick out your main strengths - those skills and attributes you know you have mastered. You will know these from your C.V. and from those in the chapter *What Are Employers Looking For?* with which you identified, e.g. reliability, adaptability, honesty, work well in a team, motivated, good communication skills, enthusiasm, culturally sensitive, and so on.

What are your limitations?

We covered this briefly in the first chapter of *Part II* so you will have already given thought to this and have a prepared response. Finish by saying that you believe none of your limitations would affect your performance.

What skills do you bring to the job? or Why should we employ you? or What makes you feel you can do this job?

Answer in terms of relevant experience, skills, enthusiasm, ability to get on with people, maturity, etc. In other words, summarise your suitability.

What are your personal/outside interests and why?

The interviewer is seeking to 'fill-in' the other side of you, to ensure your well-roundedness. Make sure you give prior thought to why you have certain interests and involvements.

What things do you enjoy in your job?

Reiterate the things that make you enthusiastic - is it the challenge of new problems, helping the public, being at the nerve-centre of activity, working alone and then connecting with the team, contributing to the 'big picture'?

What things do you enjoy least?

Be careful not to give the impression that you don't handle pressure well. You could mention slow patches, or bureaucracy, or not delivering on time to a customer because of delays beyond your control - things that most employers would also find frustrating. Be prepared to answer how you would respond to those situations.

Here are some other questions you might be asked. Plan a response to the ones you feel are most relevant and practise these in your mock interview.

What do you think/know of our organisation?

What have been some of your achievements?

Describe your management style.

How do you go about planning and/or managing time?

How much would you like to earn?

What are your salary expectations?

What is your marital status/do you have dependants?

How is your health?

What would be your perfect job?

How do you think a client should be treated?

What self-improvement learning do you do?

Why are we in business?

Who's responsible for our success?

What is your attitude to working beyond 9 to 5?

How do you see your role?

What is your educational background?

Do you have a current drivers licence/your own vehicle?

What are your qualifications?

What specialised courses have you attended?

When could you start?

Outline your personal goals for this year.

How do you react under pressure?

What qualities do you think we should be looking for?

What are some of the difficulties of being a _____ and how would you overcome them?

What are your expectations for this job?

Give me an example of how you have provided good customer service.

Describe a stressful situation for you.

What experience have you had of working with people from other cultures?

Give me an example of how you set priorities.

How do you deal with someone who is not performing?

Give me an example of how you solve problems.

How do you deal with disappointment?

What was the most rewarding event in your career - why?

What was the most disappointing event in your career - why?

What experience have you had in developing new ideas?

What is your attitude to quality? Safety?

What do you see as the most important personal asset requirement to be successful in our business?

What preparation have you done for this interview?

What current issues do you feel strongly about?

How do you deal with conflict?

Don't skip these questions! Remember to ask yourself, "how much do I want this job?" and then get stuck in!

What do you do if you are asked a question you feel is highly inappropriate or irrelevant? What should you do? This can be an awkward situation. Firstly, take time to think about your response. There are three broad options.

1. You can state outright, without aggression, that you feel the question is not relevant to the position and that therefore you do not wish to answer it. Say no more. Let the interviewer take the next step. This can be a risky option but if you feel strongly about the inappropriateness, you may feel it's worth it.

2. You can decide on a compromise answer, giving the interviewer some information you feel comfortable releasing but not other personal details you feel are private.

3. You can ask the interviewer for what purpose they want this particular information or respond with "Are you concerned that I might not be available when you need me?", for example.

There is a fourth option; that is to answer the question regardless of how you feel about it. This can often make you feel uncomfortable, stifling the rest of the interview, and can also make you feel angry at the employer.

What do you do if you don't understand a question? Don't panic. Rather than pretend you know the answer, ask for elaboration or clarification - "Do you mean ...?". or "Could you explain what you mean by ...?" If you really don't know the answer, say so and try to have an intelligent guess.

For the interview as a whole, a useful strategy is to stress positive job-related skills *periodically* during the interview and de-emphasise any experiences that might be interpreted as negative.

While this may seem daunting, the more interviews you have, the easier it gets. That's why practice is so important. One technique is to set up a mock interview.

Mock interviews

After you have prepared answers to the above questions and practised them a few times, ask someone you trust to take you through a mock interview. Give them the list of questions, the job notice, job description and your C.V., and take the whole exercise seriously from start to finish. Get them to note down anything they feel you did wrong, such as annoying speech patterns (saying "umm" or "you know" too often), repetitive gestures (looking at the ceiling for inspiration - one I have been guilty of!), too short an answer or too lengthy, and so on. Those comments will be vital to improving your performance.

Better still, if you can manage it, have the mock interview videoed. To watch your own performance is probably the most revealing method available of identifying shortcomings.

Does all this sound like too much trouble? How much do you want the job?

Questions and mock interviews

There are many questions listed in this chapter and through practising your responses to them, you should know them well. Practise your responses either in mock interviews or in your room, anywhere, time and again until you feel confident. This is one of the most important forms of preparation you can do.

16 *What questions should I ask?*

Invariably, interviewers expect applicants to ask questions about the job and about the organisation. They want to be asked questions that demonstrate your understanding of the position, clarify areas of confusion, and search for comprehension of the "big picture" or macro environment, i.e. the organisation as a whole, its growth plans, the industry, and so on. Empathise with the employer and show that you understand what they want. Not only will such information seeking be favourably received but it will also add greatly to your understanding of the job, how/where it fits in, and what the overall work environment is like.

Employers are also keen on questions about the prospects for the position, where it might lead. And it would also be wise to ask them what their expectations of the person would be, if this hasn't already been made clear. Again, this will cement your perception and understanding of the position.

Most interviewers would expect some questions on terms and conditions, employee benefits, etc. A word of caution: while it is your right to know about things like holidays, pay, hours, etc, and unfortunate that more employers don't volunteer this information at the interview, it can turn some interviewers off. My advice would be that if the basic terms and conditions have not yet been made available to you (say, in the Job Description), then ask, but leave it until the end of the interview almost as an after-thought following the more important questions.

Some other things you might like to know:

- Why is the job vacant?
- To whom would you be responsible?
- What staff training opportunities are there?
- How secure is the position?
- Questions about the organisation's clients.
- The experience/expertise of the manager to whom you would be responsible.
- When will I know the outcome of the interview?

It is wise, and will be well received, to have something prepared. For instance, to have questions written next to items on the job description that need clarification. Even if you look at it and say, "It seems the questions I had noted to ask have all been answered", at least it shows you came prepared.

Ask about

- The vacancy - clarifying areas of confusion, how the job fits in the overall organisation
- The organisation - its goals, growth plans
- Prospects
- Their expectations of the appointed person
- Conditions (leave until last)
- Why the job is vacant
- Responsibilities
- Staff training
- Job security
- Clients
- Experience of superior
- When you will know the outcome

17 *What mistakes could I make at the interview?*

The four most significant barriers to success that applicants present are:

- Lack of confidence
- Poor personal presentation
- Lack of homework about the job
- Lack of homework about the organisation

You should work hard to overcome these four barriers.

Another important barrier is poor communication skills. This is linked to some of the above - if you're lacking confidence you are not likely to say much. Communication also involves listening skills and applicants should take care to listen to the questions being asked and get *involved* in the interview.

A further obstacle, often linked to low self-confidence, can be the presence of a negative attitude or a lack of energy for the position. If you possess a negative attitude your body language, speech, responses - everything - will betray you. Fostering a positive attitude towards yourself, the job, the organisation and the whole of life, is the only real way to begin achieving. You need to own your skills and positive attributes as if they were parts of your body.

There are other kinds of barriers, some that are perhaps at the other end of the scale. Some applicants, for instance, can *oversell* themselves by talking too much or being unable to back-up claims in their application.

Talking too much is a trap you could fall into if you:

- don't really know the answer to a question
- are nervous
- know a great deal about the question but don't know where to draw the line. This may be a case of either disciplining yourself to answer the question asked or asking the interviewer "Would you like me to expand on that or any part of it?" This shows the interviewer you have more knowledge to give and that they can give you more time on the higher priority questions.

Some other things to avoid in the interview include:

- lack of technical or in-depth knowledge
- being argumentative
- having your priorities wrong (e.g. more interested in the dollars than the job)
- answering dishonestly
- sitting on the edge of the seat ready to rush out the door once the interview is over
- flippancy or inappropriate joking
- asking no questions
- no eye contact
- unhygienic (e.g. dirty fingernails) - particularly if you are applying for a job in the food industry
- not knowing specifically why you want the job

Mistakes - applicant

- **Lack of confidence**
- **Poor personal presentation**
- **Lack of homework (job and organisation)**
- **Poor communication skills**
- **Negative attitude**
- **Overselling**
- **Talking too much**
- **Others as listed at the end of the chapter**

18 What mistakes might the interviewer make?

While the interviewer has the upper hand in terms of power over the candidate, most admit to being far less than perfect.

Here are some barriers to effective interviewing:

- Doing things that underline the interviewer's power, such as:
  - a formal or authoritative manner, which may include 'talking down' to the applicant, intimidating them and leaving them tense.
  - making no effort to relax the applicant or build an atmosphere conducive to good discussion.
  - a bad seating arrangement which is often one akin to an interrogation, e.g. a desk between the interviewer and the applicant which acts as a barrier and underlines the interviewer's dominance.
  - overdressing by the interviewer.

- Talking too much. Sometimes the interviewer may talk too much about specifics and give the applicant an overload of information. Occasionally, they may ask long-winded questions, which may stem from inadequate preparation for the interview or insufficient knowledge of the vacancy.

- Allowing insufficient time for the applicant to respond. This may be due to too many questions for the allotted time, lack of interest in the candidate, or a general lack of interviewing experience.

- Interruptions. Taking phone calls or leaving the interview room.

- Jargon-talk. Every industry has its own language. It should not be assumed that applicants know it.

- Too many interviewers. A panel of more than six is extremely intimidating. It will be difficult for the candidate to feel at ease and respond with confidence.

- Personal bias, prejudices, stereotyping or cultural insensitivity.

These are the main ones but also watch for:

- An assumption that the applicant understands the company/organisation
- Poor listening skills or inattention
- Too informal
- Negative attitude (yes, interviewers can have these as well!)
- Not asking in-depth questions or probing further
- Being unnecessarily nosy
- Being disorganised ("Now where did I put that application?")
- Not volunteering basic information on pay, holidays, other conditions of work

Once aware of the barriers, which many interviewers seem to be, they will probably try to overcome them, but at least you, as an applicant, can recognise them. This will give you some degree of power to overcome or control the effects.

However, be aware that occasionally some of these barriers may be used deliberately to see how an applicant functions under extreme stress. Hopefully this will not become a widespread practice but in some fields (upper management levels) it may be an appropriate strategy. Verbal barriers may also be used deliberately to control the interview - this is important when discussion strays off the track.

Think about how you would handle each of these barriers if presented with them at an interview. Work out a strategy for dealing with the main ones and practise this in the mock interview.

Mistakes - interviewer

- Authoritative manner
- Poor seating arrangement
- Talking too much
- Jargon
- Personal prejudice
- Insufficient time for applicant to respond
- Others as listed

- Failure to relax applicant
- Overdressing
- Interruptions
- Too many on panel

19 *After the interview*

First of all - YOU SURVIVED!!

You can expect to be contacted within a specified timeframe, usually within two weeks. To wait any longer than this is unsatisfactory and you should ring and ask if a decision has been made and when you can expect to hear. I have applied for positions (two come to mind) for which no contact was ever made after the interview. I count myself lucky not to have worked for such incompetent employers. The majority, fortunately, do not fall into this category.

You may receive a phone call and/or a letter advising you one way or the other. If you are the chosen applicant, you will probably be telephoned first and offered the position.

Generally, no feedback on the interview or application is given but many employers are happy to give you feedback on performance if you ask. Some, however, will not, feeling they are setting themselves up for trouble. If this is the case, there is little you can do.

Finally, once you walk out of the interview, it's over. You did the best you could. You might recognise where you could have done better but there is no point in worrying about it now. No job interview is worth an ulcer. However, when you feel ready, try to write down the questions you were asked and the responses you gave. This may help for future interviews. If you are aware of questions you did not answer well, note them down and give special attention to them prior to your next interview.

And if you don't get the job? Put it down to experience, nurse your bruised ego back to health, get stuck into those affirmations, and try, try, try, again!

Afterwards

- Expect to be contacted within a fortnight
- If it's longer than a fortnight, ring and ask
- You will most likely be telephoned if you are first choice
- Generally no feedback given but ask if you want it
- Forget about the interview once it's over
- Try to analyse where you think you went wrong
- Nurse yourself back to positivity if you missed out

20 *Final choice factors*

What are those factors that help employers make their final choice?

Clearly, it is how the candidates rated against the critical factors that has the most bearing on the final choice. It's a simple question of "Who best can do the job?". Everything is taken into account from the application through to the candidate's interview performance.

Employers will also want to feel confident about the candidate's adaptability, compatibility, enthusiasm, and how they will enhance the organisation.

Work history and experience, qualifications, communication skills, attitude, and personality (and those other important attributes already stated) are important influences. If there is a stalemate between two or more applicants, the employer may contact the referees (if he/she has not already done so) to obtain information that could tip the scales. If they can't decide, they may hold a second interview.

Significant too is the employer's own intuition, attitude and concept of a 'good employee', sometimes referred to as a 'gut feeling'. In fact, in the end, these aspects will probably be the strongest influence after consideration of other factors.

Another influence on their final choice may be how others in the organisation responded to the person, such as the receptionist, or those who may have met the person prior to the interview when they were being shown around. Their comments will be taken into account.

Remember, often the differences between applicants are paper thin. Don't think badly of yourself if you miss out.

Final choice

Affected by:

- **Critical factors**
- **Application through to interview performance**
- **Adaptability**
- **Compatibility**
- **Enthusiasm**
- **How you will enhance the organisation**

- **Work history and experience**
- **Referees**
- **Employer's 'gut feeling'**
- **Others in the organisation who may have met you**

Don't think badly of yourself if you missed out!